# I AM WHO I BELIEVE I AM!

## EMPOWERING AFFIRMATIONS AND CONTEMPLATIONS FOR CHILDREN.

### M. E. FORBES

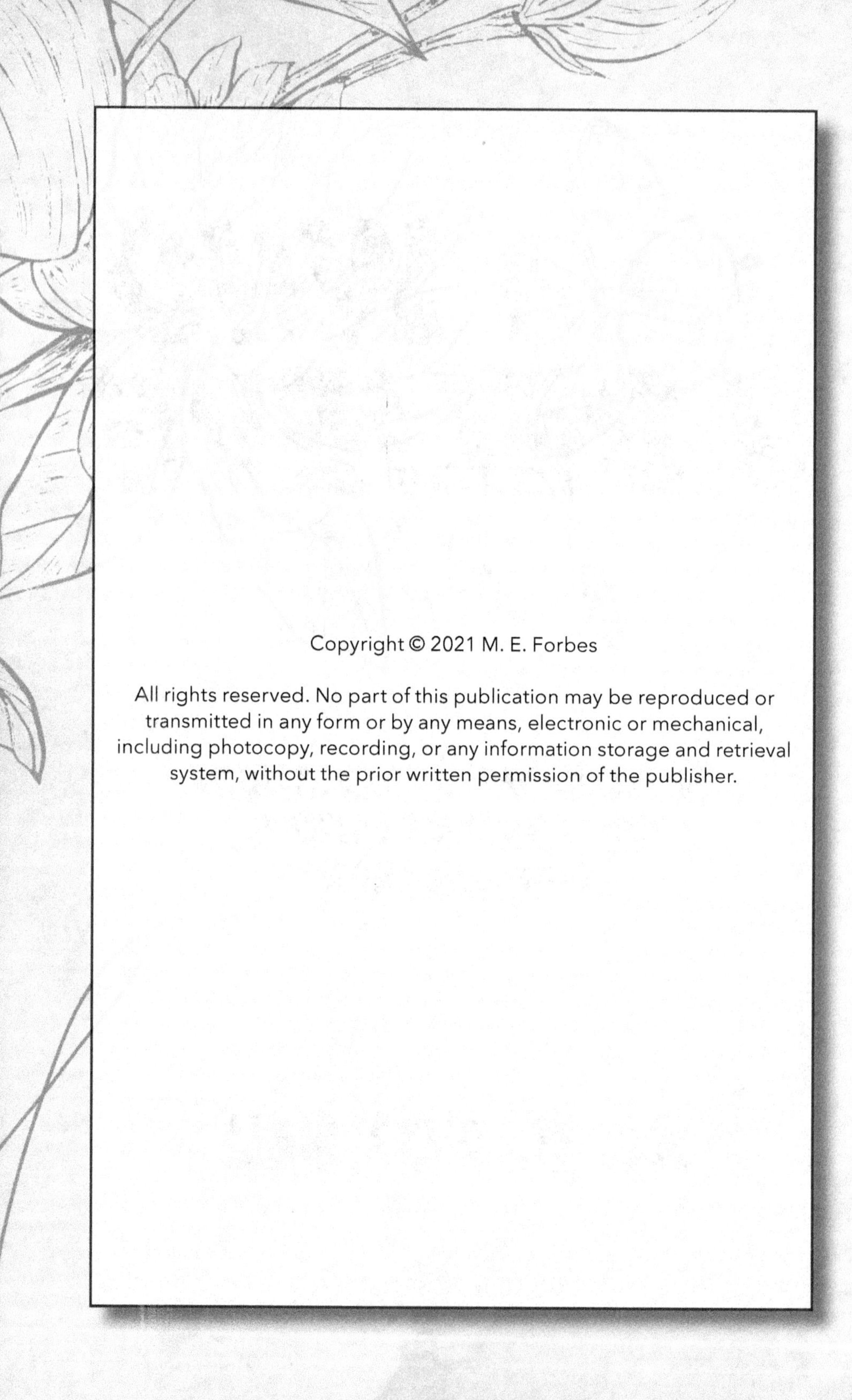

This collection is lovingly dedicated to my daughter.
Thank you
for being my inspiration, my motivation,
my teacher, my best friend.

# ACKNOWLEDGMENT

My eternal gratitude to
Brenda T. Guzman
&
Riley Richards,
whose help made this collection
infinitely better than it would have otherwise been.

# CONTENTS

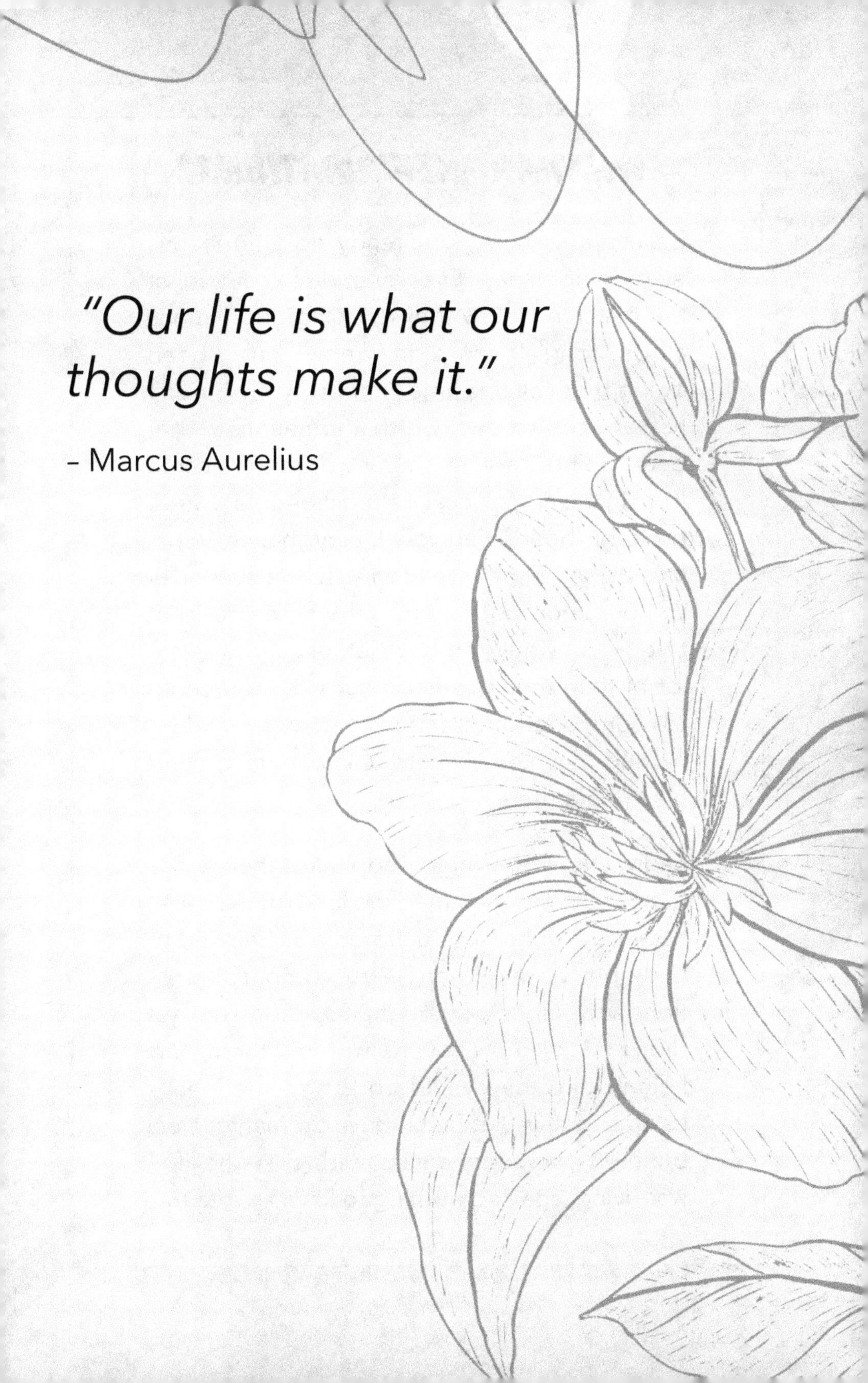

*"Our life is what our thoughts make it."*

– Marcus Aurelius

# WHAT ARE AFFIRMATIONS?

Believe it or not, you already do affirmations every single day. Everyone does, but most people don't know they're doing affirmations all day long. If you didn't know you've been doing them all this time, you probably haven't had any control over which affirmations you've been doing, or even know where they came from in the first place. Like most people, you've probably been living your life by chance, hope, and wishes. That's like leaving home every day without knowing how to get where you want to go. You would quickly get lost and waste a lot of time trying to find your way. You could ask someone for directions, but you would be hoping they know where you want to go and how to get there.

Sadly, this is how most people live their entire lives, and for a long time, I did too. After a while, however, I got really frustrated and decided to find a better way. When I learned about affirmations and self-talk, I thought it sounded crazy. I didn't think I knew anyone who did them, and I didn't think they would work. It seemed really hard, and it was at first. I gave up many times, but then I would try again. I didn't like the life I was living, so I had nothing to lose. I wrote this

book to help you understand what I wish someone had told me a long time ago.

## Why are affirmations important?

First, let's look at what exactly an affirmation is.
To affirm something is to say or show it's true.
That means everything you say or think about
yourself is an affirmation. If you think you can't
do something, then guess what? You've just
affirmed it; that's an affirmation. If you think
you can do something, that's an affirmation
too. Every time someone says you're smart or
really good at something, they are affirming it,
and if you hear that often enough, your subconscious mind will accept it as truth, and it
will become part of your identity. Every time
someone says you're not good at something, or
calls you stupid, they're affirming those things,
and if repeated often enough, your subconscious mind will accept them, making them part
of your identity as well. It's important to know
what affirmations are, because affirmations are
important.

A simple way to think of affirmations is as a form
of self-talk; the things you believe, think, and
say about yourself. Those ideas are very powerful because you are very powerful. You are so

powerful, you can create your reality with your beliefs, your thoughts, and your words. Your beliefs, which you may not even be aware of, are responsible for your thoughts. Your thoughts lead to your feelings, which direct your words and actions, causing your experiences. The world around you then responds to your words and actions. It all begins with your beliefs (the cause) and ends with what you experience in life (the effect). You can think of everything you experience as a fruit, and the beliefs which start it all are the seeds from which the whole tree grew. The fruit you get is determined by the seeds you plant.

You may be familiar with the placebo effect. This happens when someone is given a pill and they're told it will do something such as heal an illness or relief pain. In studies, the pill is sometimes a fake. It can't do anything, but some people who take it still get better. That's because our beliefs can influence our immune system, causing some people to heal themselves just by believing they have been given a medication or medical procedure when the truth is, they hadn't. Those people truly believed they would be cured, so their subconscious mind made it happen.

The affirmations in this book are both observations of who you are now, and proclamations of who you will become. They are tools to create the life you want and become the person you choose to be. That's because when you say or hear something about yourself over and over, the part of your mind which controls most of your life will accept it as both the truth and a command. It will then use this information to run your life and create your future reality. Your mind will even ignore anything which disagrees with what it believes.

If you believe you can't do something, it will be very difficult if not impossible for you to do because your mind will keep finding ways to make it difficult. Think about how many distractions you find when you don't want to do something, or how much harder you have to work at something you believe is difficult. On the other hand, if you expect something to be easy, or you simply enjoy doing it, you may find you have no trouble doing it, while someone else may find it difficult.

What you believe about yourself matters. Can you think of some things you believe about yourself? Do you always find proof that these things are true? Do you remember what or who caused you to believe those things in the first place? Do those beliefs make you happy or sad?

It is challenging to recognize many of your own beliefs because they may have been so deep in the subconscious part of your mind for so long, that you accept them as basic facts rather than things you choose to, or were told to believe. You may not be aware of them, but they're there, always in the background, controlling every part of your life. The only way to get rid of the ones you don't want is to replace them with ones you do want. That's what affirmations help you do.

## How this book can change your life.

I wrote this book to help you understand how powerful you are. You can create the life you want! On the following pages, you'll find positive and powerful affirmations followed by contemplations, which are thoughts about the affirmations for you to consider. I suggest that each morning, you read an affirmation and the contemplation, then think about it throughout the day. Consider how you feel about the topic and what it means to you; you may remember a situation related to the affirmation, or imagine how it might apply to your life in the future.

Throughout your day, you'll find chances to practice the affirmation, or proof that you already do. You can also discuss it with friends during the day, and with your family in the evening. I also suggest reading it again in bed at night, giving your subconscious mind an opportunity to take it in as you sleep.

Affirmations don't have to reflect your reality right now. If one is not true for you yet, but you say it often enough, your subconscious mind will help you achieve it. A good way to help your subconscious mind accept an affirmation is to repeat it out loud in a joyful manner as if it has already happened, and you're now happily stating a fact or excitedly telling a friend. Yes, it will feel weird at first, but you can do it when there's no one around. It may feel as if you're lying to yourself, but there is a big difference between a lie and an affirmation. A lie, even to yourself, is trying to convince the conscious mind something is what it's not, while an affirmation is a command to the subcon-scious mind to create the reality you choose to experience. You were born with this ability; it's part of who you are, and you're meant to use it, which is why everyone does it naturally every single day. Affirmations are truly a natural part of being human; most people are just not aware they have this ability and can control it.

Emotions add extra power to affirmations because your subconscious mind actually understands feelings more than words. It also communicates in images rather than words, so as you say your affirmations, imagine them being absolutely true, and feel as you will feel when they are. If you do all of these things every day, you will surely notice a difference in your life, and more important, in yourself.

If you read one affirmation in this book each day and go in order, it will take you almost four months to read them all. Then, you can start all over again. Another way to read this book is to randomly pick an affirmation each day. A third option is to choose the affirmation which will help you the most on a particular day, depending on what you're feeling. There are several things which help affirmations to be effective. I will go over these at the end of this book, but for now, just remember repetition is very important; each time you send a message to your subconscious mind, you increase the chance of that message becoming a belief which will be acted on. That's why you will notice some ideas are repeated throughout this book. That's also why it's a good idea to think about each affirmation all through the day, and read this book more than just once.

"You are today where
your thoughts have
brought you; you will be
tomorrow where your
thoughts take you."

– James Allen

# I AM UNIQUE!

In a universe of **countless** wonders and miracles, on a planet with billions of people, I am the only me; the only one there will ever be. That makes me one of a kind; precious and important. I am grateful and happy to be me!

# I AM HAPPILY WHOLE AND COMPLETE!

I am me as I'm meant to be. I am whole and complete, precious and perfect to fulfill my destiny. I don't need anyone or anything to make me happy or complete.

# I AM A PRECIOUS GIFT TO THE WORLD WITH A PRECIOUS GIFT FOR THE WORLD.

I am a precious one-of-a-kind gift to the world. There will never be another me. I was born to do something amazing no one else can do. I may not know what that is yet, but I will figure it out when the time is just right. That's why I listen to the small voice inside and always follow my heart.

# I HONOR THE DIVINE IN ALL BEINGS.

Everyone is special and important. We are all equal, even though each of us is having a different experience, so I treat everyone with love and respect.

# I TAKE PRIDE IN BEING HONEST AND TRUSTWORTHY.

My words and actions tell the world who I am. To tell a lie would be to dishonor my true self. Lies come from fear, which is the opposite of love, so I only speak truth, and always with love.

# I AM CAPABLE!

With focus and practice, I can do amazing things. Some things will be easier for me than others, but I will achieve everything I truly believe I can, as long as I keep trying.

# I AM LIKE THE SUN!

The sun always shines, but sometimes we can't see it because of clouds. When the clouds go away, we can see the bright and beautiful sun again. My feelings and moods are like the clouds; I let them come and go. They are not who I am. Who I am is always bright and beautiful, shining like the sun. Who I am is always positive and loving. Who I am is not determined by anyone or anything outside of me. Whatever happens, I will be loving, grateful, and forgiving with myself and everyone else.

# I QUICKLY TELL SOMEONE IF I DON'T FEEL SAFE.

I am surrounded by people who love me. If I don't feel safe, there is always someone to help me. If I need help, I will ask for it.

# I AM ALWAYS HAPPY TO SHARE.

When I share the things which make me happy, I help others be happy too. Then there is more happiness and love around me.

# I EXPECT GOOD THINGS.

Good things happen every day. I can't always know what's going to happen, but I always know it's going to be good for me somehow. I won't always understand it, but I know everything that happens *to* me really happens *for* me, and it's all good!

# I LOVE KEEPING MY BODY CLEAN, HEALTHY, AND STRONG.

Being healthy is important for having a long and happy life, so I take care of my body every day. I eat mostly healthy foods and drink lots of water. I get plenty of exercise every day, and enough sleep every night.

# I AM SO MUCH BIGGER THAN FEAR!

Fear is a feeling which helps me when my body may be in danger. I am not my body, and when my body is safe, I don't need to be afraid. Fear is almost always about what could happen in the future. That's worrying. Worrying means I'm ignoring the present moment because I'm trying to predict the future, and it's usually a future I don't want. Worrying can make my body sick. Instead of worrying, I can choose to be present and positive. I can choose to do the best I can in each moment. I can choose to think only about what I want to happen, and expect the future I intend to have. Being positive and expecting the best lifts me up above worrying, and makes me bigger and stronger than fear.

# I AM RESPONSIBLE FOR MY FEELINGS AND BEHAVIOR.

When something happens, that's all there is to it until I choose to judge it; to call it good or bad, which only means if it makes me happy or not. If I don't judge or label something, then it just is. When something happens, I can count to three and decide if I want to judge, label, and react, or accept that what happened is already in the past. Then I can choose to respond to it in a loving way without judgement or fear.

# I AM INTELLIGENT.

I am very smart, and getting smarter every day. I enjoy learning and using new knowledge in my life, but I don't need to know everything. Just as a fish doesn't need to know how to climb a tree, I only need to know the things which will help me be the best me I can be, and do exactly what I am here to do.

# I AM QUIETLY EXTRAORDINARY.

I know a little extra effort makes a big difference, so every day, in everything I do, I try a little harder; I do a little more than I have to. I expect more from myself, so I can give more to the world. Adding a little extra when I do ordinary things makes me extraordinary.

# I JOYFULLY CELEBRATE THE ACHIEVEMENTS OF OTHERS.

When someone does something wonderful, I am happy for them because I know it feels good to do something well, especially when it took a lot of work. It's fun to support each other, and help each other do even more.

# I TAKE PRIDE IN DOING WHAT I SAY I WILL.

I do my best to keep my promises so everyone knows they can always trust me to do what I say I will. When I can't do something, they know I did my best.

# I AM NATURALLY JOYFUL!

I am always filled with joy. Joy is different from happiness. Joy is bigger than happiness, and comes from deep inside me when I am being my true self and I am grateful for all the blessings in my life.

# I OBEY MY PARENTS.

I am very blessed to be loved, supported, and taken care of. I am very grateful for my family, so I do my best every day to obey and honor my parents.

# I RADIATE LOVE AND JOY.

I send out thoughts and feelings of love, happiness, and peace into the world. I also like to think thankful thoughts for all the blessings around me every day. With my thoughts and feelings, I am making a difference in the world.

# I AM WORTHY OF LOVE.

I am always kind, helpful, and loving, and that's exactly how I deserve to be treated. I am worthy of love, and I only spend time with people who appreciate and respect me. I am not rude or hurtful to anyone, and I will not let anyone be rude or hurtful to me.

# I AM MY OWN BEST FRIEND.

I respect and take care of myself. I enjoy being with others, but I am happy alone too. I spend time with myself so I can know and love myself.

# I AM ALWAYS MINDFUL AND CAREFUL.

If I'm not mindful and careful, I may get hurt, so I always pay attention to what and who are around me, and I only stay where I feel safe. When I don't feel safe, I tell an adult I trust.

# I AM CONFIDENT.

Everyone is different, and everyone is good at things related to their destiny, so I don't need to compare myself to anyone else. I am happy. I am intelligent. I am loving. I am capable. I am the only me there will ever be, and perfect just as I am.

# I AM SO BLESSED AND GRATEFUL TO BE SURROUNDED BY PEOPLE WHO LOVE ME.

I am so blessed! There is so much love all around me! I have many wonderful people in my life who love and support me, and I love them too!

# I AM PATIENT.

I know everything that happens to me really happens *for* me. That means I may not always get what I want, but I always have just what I need in every moment. When I don't get something I want, I know there is always a reason, so I am patient and grateful that I only get what's best for me.

# I ENJOY CHALLENGES.

Growing means trying new things. Some of them may be difficult at first, and some may be scary too, but challenges are opportunities for me to be creative and figure out how to solve problems. Every challenge makes me stronger, smarter, and better.

# I AM A WONDERFUL FRIEND.

Friends are special blessings who make life even better. I am very grateful for all the wonderful friends I have, and I am always a wonderful friend to them.

# I CHOOSE MY ATTITUDE.

How I feel about someone or something that's happening is very important. My feelings affect my thoughts, my body, and my behavior. My mood affects everyone around me and how they treat me. Being in a bad mood could cause me to be hurtful to the people I love, or miss out on some of the fun and joy of life. When I'm in a good mood, it's easier for me to help others feel good too. It also helps me think positive thoughts, have more energy, and enjoy life a lot more. Being in a good mood doesn't mean I have to be happy all the time; it means I'm positive even when things don't go the way I wish they would. My mood and attitude are very important, so I never let anything or anyone else determine how I feel. I always choose my attitude.

# I AM DRAWN TO THINGS WHICH WILL HELP ME SHARE MY GIFT.

The things I find most fascinating are likely to be the things which will help me develop and share my gift with the world. They are the things I am naturally good at and drawn to. Other people will be better than I am at other things because those things will help them develop and share their own gifts. We each have a different gift to share with the world, so we're all good at different things.

# I ALWAYS DO THE RIGHT THING.

Every day, I have choices, and because I follow my heart instead of what others are doing, I always do what's right for me. The world knows who I am by what I say and do, so I only say what I know is true, and always do what I know is right.

# I GIVE AND DESERVE RESPECT.

I am always respectful to others. I also respect myself, and will not allow anyone to disrespect me. I will stay away from people who are not nice to me, and if anyone talks to me, touches me, or treats me in any way that makes me feel uncomfortable, I will loudly tell them to stop, and I will tell an adult I trust. I deserve to be respected.

# I AM ALWAYS HAPPY TO HELP OTHERS.

Everyone needs help sometimes. I am surrounded by people who are always there for me when I need help, and I am always happy to help others.

# I ALWAYS SPEAK AND ACT WITH LOVE.

What I put out into the world comes back to me. The way I treat others is how they will treat me, so I always speak and act with love.

# I AM LIVING PEACEFULLY IN THIS MOMENT.

My mind is very powerful and active. It likes to spend a lot of time remembering the past or worrying about the future. It likes to think the same thoughts over and over, day after day. I control and calm my busy mind by keeping it focused on this moment. This helps me enjoy and appreciate my life instead of wasting it remembering, worrying, or repeating. It also helps me to think more clearly and creatively, feel more relaxed and happy, and send love out into the world. My mind is very powerful, but I control it.

# I KNOW EVERYTHING HAPPENS FOR A REASON.

I don't understand why some things happen, but I know everything happens for a reason, and it's always good. Even when something seems bad, I know something good can come from it. Sometimes I have to look for the good, and sometimes I just have to be patient, but there is always good.

# I SEE EVERYONE IS AMAZING.

Because I live from my heart, I see everyone is as unique and precious as I am. We are all living miracles, full of love and capable of great things. Everyone is different, but no one is better than anyone else. Everyone is amazing!

# I FIND BEAUTY EVERYWHERE.

There's so much beauty everywhere! Sometimes it's a breathtaking sunset, or a full moon so big it seems close enough to touch. Sometimes beauty is small and unexpected, like a baby's smile, or a cute tiny flower growing in a crack in the sidewalk. Sometimes it's the feeling inside when my heart is so full of love, it spills out my eyes as tears of joy. Every day, in so many ways, life is always rejoicing around me.

# I APPRECIATE COMPLIMENTS, BUT I DON'T NEED THEM.

I feel good when someone says something nice about me, and I always say "Thank you", but I don't need someone to say something nice about me to feel good. I am always happy just being me. I like myself just the way I am, so if someone says something nice about me, I'm okay, and if they say something about me that's not nice, I'm still okay. I'm happy being me no matter what someone else thinks or says.

# I ALWAYS LOOK FOR THE GOOD.

The subconscious part of my mind is very powerful, and is always looking for ways to prove what I believe. It works hard to help me get just what I need or expect. That's why I expect and look for the good in everyone and everything, everywhere, every day.

# I GLADLY APOLOGIZE WHEN I NEED TO.

I know I am perfect just as I am for what I was born to do, and everything works out for the best, but sometimes things happen that I don't mean to happen, and sometimes I say or do things which may hurt someone else. When those things happen, I always say "I'm sorry". That lets the other person know I didn't mean to say or do anything hurtful, and that I'm sorry they got hurt or upset because of something I did or said. Saying "I'm sorry" makes us both feel better.

# I ADJUST EASILY TO NEW SITUATIONS.

Things are always changing. That's just part of life, but it's exciting, because change means new adventures, new things to learn, and sometimes new friends too! Even though new things can be scary sometimes, I always adjust to changes and look forward to new experiences.

# I AM A MINDFUL LISTENER.

When someone is talking to me, I always look at them and listen carefully to what they are saying. That's the best way to be sure I understand what they are saying. Even if I already know what they are telling me, I listen anyway, because I may learn something new. If I have questions, I always ask.

# I WAKE UP HAPPY EVERY MORNING.

Life is truly wonderful! I wake up happy and grateful every morning, excited about the new adventures and opportunities the day has for me. There are always new wonders to discover, new things to learn, and new ways to have fun!

# I AM TRULY CAPABLE OF MORE THAN CAN BE IMAGINED!

I am intelligent, creative, and strong. I am capable of anything I focus on and really try to do. I am especially drawn to the things I need to learn and be good at so I can share my gift with the world. By following my heart and doing what comes naturally, rather than competing with others or trying to please someone else, I will do things the world has never seen because no one else could have done them.

# I ENJOY BEING KIND TO OTHERS.

I like being kind to others. When we are kind to each other, everyone feels better. Being kind is a joyful and easy way to make the world a better place.

# I AM EXACTLY WHO I NEED TO BE, TO DO WHAT I'M HERE TO DO.

We need each other. Everyone is here with something special to share with the world. We can't do what we're here to do if we waste our lives comparing ourselves to others and competing with them. I don't try to be like anyone else. I am exactly who I need to be to do what I'm here to do.

# I FIND JOY IN EVERYTHING I DO.

How I think and feel about the things I do makes a difference in how well I do them, and how much I enjoy doing them. I do everything the best I can, and I always find a way to make it fun, even if I don't really want to do it. When I finish doing something, I know I did my best, and had a good time too.

# I ALWAYS HAVE A CHOICE.

Every day, I get to choose what I think about; what I feel; what I say, and how I do the things I do. When something happens, I can take a deep breath and choose how to respond. I always have a choice, and I always choose to be positive and kind.

# I AM PART OF AN ABUNDANT UNIVERSE!

All around me, there is more than enough of everything; from sand on the beaches and blossoms on the trees, to stars in the sky. More than I need is always available to me, so I don't need to be selfish or compete with others. The universe is abundant and always provides for us.

# I FORGIVE EASILY.

Being angry with someone for a long time is not good for me. It does not come from a place of love, and it keeps me from being happy. I don't have to like someone who is hurtful, but I will forgive them so I can be happy and enjoy my life.

# I LOVE TO READ.

I love learning. The more I know, the better I understand the world we live in and the people around me. Also, the more I know, the more creative I can be. Learning from others helps me to think of things no one has thought of yet. I am already very smart, and reading helps me get smarter every day.

# I AM PART OF ONE BIG FAMILY, AND EARTH IS OUR HOME.

My family is made up of different people, but we're all connected and love each other. Every living thing on Earth is connected. We all live together on this planet, which is our home, and every living thing adds something important to the world. Every animal is intelligent in its own way, and does something amazing which helps us all. Every plant is precious, providing food for us or other animals, cleaning the air we breathe, keeping our soil in place and healthy, keeping the earth cool, or providing medicine for us when we get sick. Everyone and everything is important, and together we're one big Earth family.

# I GIVE WHAT I WANT.

I treat everyone the way I want to be treated, and always send loving thoughts out into the world, because that's what will come back to me. I am honest, loving, and helpful, so that's the kind of people I attract in my life. Even when someone is not nice to me, I am still nice to them. Everything I want for myself, I give to the world.

# I LOVE BEING ME!

I accept, respect, forgive, and love myself just as I am. I have many wonderful qualities and abilities, and I love the things which make me unique. I do not try to fit in with others. I do not need anyone to approve of me, because no one is better than I am. I will not change who I am so others will like me. I am happy being me, and I am going to have an amazing life!

# I AM WORTHY AND GRATEFUL.

I attract and get what I truly believe I deserve. I know I am worthy of good things, and I am grateful for the many blessings in my life, and the countless more to come.

# I FOCUS ON WHAT I CAN'T SEE.

I am grateful for the things I have. They make life easy or comfortable, and are helpful or fun to have, but I know material things only make life easier; they don't make up my life. The things which really matter aren't made of matter at all. They are things like love, good health, joy, and peace. These are the things I choose to focus on every day.

# I DO WHAT'S RIGHT; NOT WHAT'S EASY.

I matter; everything I do matters, and how I do them matter too because it's a reflection of me. How I do small things will become how I do bigger things until it becomes how I do everything, so I only do what's right, and I always do the very best I can. That makes me happy and I don't have to apologize or make excuses.

# I AM ALWAYS FAIR.

I treat others the way I want to be treated. If I'm not honest and fair, others will not be honest and fair with me. No one likes someone they can't trust, so I show I can be trusted by always telling the truth and being kind to everyone.

# I EXPECT MIRACLES.

I am a living miracle, and I know there are wonders and miracles all around me every day. Many are so common, some people stop seeing them. Some are so small, most people don't notice them at all. I take time to notice and enjoy the little wonders and the great miracles of life, and it makes me happy and grateful to know I am one too!

# I AM OKAY EITHER WAY.

I will not always get what I want, but I always have more than I need, and I know everything happens for my good. When I don't get what I want, I just need to be patient and expect something even better. That's why whether or not I get what I want, I am always okay.

# I HAVE A GREAT IMAGINATION.

I am very creative. I can imagine amazing things. I think of interesting stories, fun songs, and beautiful pictures. Most of all, I love to imagine how I will make the world a better place.

# I ALWAYS HAVE WHAT IT TAKES.

I am always brave, strong, ready and capable, because I am always blessed with everything I need to do whatever I need to do. Even if I don't have everything when I start, I get exactly what I need when I need it. I always have what it takes to get through everything I go through.

# I ALWAYS FIND THE POSITIVE.

Negative thoughts and hurtful words do not serve anyone, so I always find something truthful and positive to say. Sometimes it's hard, but that just makes it a fun challenge; I make a game out of it, and can surprise myself with how many truthful and positive things I can think of when I try. No matter what the situation is, there is always something good to say, and always something to be grateful for.

# I RESPECT EVERYONE'S PATH.

Everyone is on their own path, having the experiences they need to have on the way to their destiny. I can't know what someone else needs to experience to do what they are here to do, so I don't judge others. I may not agree with what someone else believes, but that doesn't make them wrong; they may just be seeing things differently because they are on a different path.

# I DECIDE WHO I AM.

I decide who I am with my beliefs, and create my life with every thought. That's why I focus on what I want, and always stay positive.

# I SAY YES!

I say yes to life. I say yes to every chance to be loving and kind. I say yes to every chance to forgive. I say yes to every chance to be helpful. I say yes to every chance to be happy. I say yes to every chance to make a positive difference in the world. I say yes!

# I HAVE FAITH.

Life is wonderful. Nothing can happen that's not supposed to, and everything happens for my good, so I don't worry. No matter what happens, I know I will be okay.

# I FLOOD THE WORLD WITH LOVE.

I live from my heart. Every day, I sit quietly, breathe deeply, and focus on my heart, sending love out into the world. I imagine my love like waves of light, radiating from my heart, rippling out in all directions. I imagine my love flowing through the walls of my home and down the street, all through town, then through cities, over mountains and oceans, warming and lighting up everyone as it moves around the world before drifting out into space.

# I ALWAYS DO THE BEST I CAN.

In everything I do, I always do the best I can. When I'm finished doing something, I never have to make excuses or feel ashamed. I always know I did my best.

# I AM EXCITED AND GRATEFUL FOR THIS DAY.

Every day is a new blessing, another day I am healthy, happy, safe, and loved in this beautiful and amazing world. Every single day, there are countless things to be excited about and thankful for.

# I GO TO BED THANKFUL AND I SLEEP PEACEFULLY.

When I go to bed at night, I think about all the wonderful things which happened that day. I send thankful thoughts into the universe for all the blessings in my life. I like to fall asleep thinking about all the things I am grateful for.

# I CAN DO THE "IMPOSSIBLE".

Every day, someone does something everyone else thought was impossible. "Impossible" only means no one has figured out how to do something yet, but one day, someone will, and that someone can be me!

# I AM MAKING THE WORLD A BETTER PLACE.

Just by being me, I am making a positive difference in the world. I am thoughtful, generous, calm, kind, and caring. I live as I would like to see everyone live, because I know that to see the change, I must first be the change.

# I KNOW MY THOUGHTS ARE POWERFUL.

What I think and believe matters. I choose to think positive thoughts, and I believe and expect only the best. Things will still happen that I don't like or want, but they won't keep me from being grateful and positive. There is love and goodness all around me every day, and because that's what I focus on, that's what I will get more of.

# I AM BLESSED, GRATEFUL, AND GENEROUS.

There is more than enough food for everyone; no one should ever be hungry. There is more than enough money for everyone; no one should be without what they need. There is more than enough love for everyone; no one should ever feel lonely. We live in an abundant universe, so I gladly share what I have and help others when I can, because the universe always gives me more than I need.

# I CHOOSE TO BE HAPPY NOW.

I choose to be happy because in this very moment, I have so much to be grateful for. I don't need to wait for something special to happen or for someone else to make me happy. I choose to be happy now, not "when..."

# I THINK ABOUT WHAT
# I THINK ABOUT.

I create my life. If I think positive and loving thoughts, I will have positive and loving feelings, I will notice good things all around me, and I will attract positive and loving people into my life. If I think negative thoughts, I will have negative feelings, see lots of negative things all around me, and attract negative people into my life. The universe gives me more of what I put out into the world, and my mind looks for more of what I focus on, so I think about what I think about, and choose to be grateful, kind, happy and loving.

## I AM CREATED BY MY PAST SO I CAN CREATE MY FUTURE.

Everything that has happened to me helped to make me who I am today, and I'm exactly who I need to be today to become the great person I will be tomorrow.

# I AM HEART-SMART AND BRAIN-SMART.

Because my heart and my brain are smart and powerful, I am both loving and intelligent. I follow my heart, but also use my brain. Together, they are an amazing team, guiding and helping me every day.

# I LOVE BEING HAPPY!

When I'm happy, my body is light and full of energy, and my mind is clear and calm. When I'm happy, I help others be happy, which makes life more fun for everyone. That's why I think positive thoughts and focus on being loving, grateful, and joyful.

# I CAN DO HARD THINGS.

My heart, body, and mind are all strong. They help me stand up when I fall; try again when I fail; learn from my mistakes, and keep getting better. Some things are easy for me, and some things are hard, but I can do hard things, even if it takes a lot of practice.

# I LIVE BY CHOICE, NOT BY CHANCE.

I can't control everything, and even if I could, I wouldn't, because if I did, I would miss out on things I can't even imagine. I do have control over my life by living by choice, with intention. I have goals, and every day, I do something to get closer to my goals. I only have one life, so I am not going to leave it up to chance, or let someone else take control of it. I live by choice.

# I GROW THROUGH CHANGE.

Life is all about growth, and growing means changing. Everything and everyone changes. Most of the time, the changes are so slow, we don't notice them, but sometimes change happens suddenly, and that can be scary. Some changes are only for a short time, but some changes are for a very long time. Change will always be part of life; nothing stays the same forever, so when things change, I choose to go through it and grow through it.

# I AM, AND THAT'S ALL I NEED TO BE.

I am alive and I am loved,
I am safe and I am healthy,
I am blessed and I am enough,
I am whole and I am worthy;
I am the one and only me,
and that is all I need to be!

# I KNOW MYSELF.

I can't truly love someone I don't know. I can't truly know someone I don't spend time with. I know who I am because I spend time with myself. I like to be mindful, being in the present moment, where I pay attention to my thoughts and feelings. I welcome them, sit with them, and question them. They are not loud like the noisy messages from outside of me. I have to sit quietly, listen, and let them guide me to truth. Knowing myself means I don't have to be who anyone else tells me to be, or do what everyone else is doing. Knowing myself helps me do what's right for me.

# I EXPECT SOMETHING BETTER.

I can only want what I know, but I don't always know everything that's available or possible. If I always get exactly what I want, I may not always get what is best. Instead, I always ask for what I want, but add "…or something better."

# I HAVE MORE TO BE THANKFUL FOR THAN I CAN EVER KNOW.

Even if all I did was say "thank you" all day long, I still could not say it enough because I have so much to be thankful for, that there isn't enough time in my whole life to even think of it all. What I can do is be grateful for all my blessings, and be a blessing to others.

# I KNOW IT'S NOT ALWAYS ABOUT ME.

When someone does something hurtful to me, I take time to think about it; I ask myself if I did anything hurtful to that person. If I did, I apologize and do what I can to make things better. I also know that most of the time, it's not about me at all. Sometimes people say or do hurtful things because they are hurting inside or don't know how to love themselves. When that happens, I forgive them and help them if I can.

# I AM LIVING A GREAT ADVENTURE!

My life is a great adventure! Because I live from my heart, I attract the people and things which help me to grow and move toward my destiny. Anyone I meet may teach me something I need to know. Any experience I have may bring me wisdom, help me to grow, or point me in the direction I need to go. There are no accidents; life is a great adventure.

# *I LOVE MYSELF!*

I am loving and worthy of love. I teach others I'm worthy of love by loving and taking care of myself. I teach others I deserve respect by showing I respect myself. I treat myself and everyone else the way I expect everyone else to treat me.

# I CAN CHANGE HOW I SEE THINGS.

The way I feel about something may be because of the information I have, or how I'm feeling at that moment. I might change my mind later, which is okay; it just means I'm learning and growing.

# I APPRECIATE ALL KINDS OF FLOWERS.

I like flowers. There are lots of different flowers, but every flower is beautiful in its own way. One flower is not better than another flower, just different; some are big and some are small; some have many petals and some have few; some smell wonderful and some have no fragrance at all; some come in lots of colors and some come in only one color; some bloom in the spring and some wait until summer. I'm glad there are so many different flowers, because if there was only one flower, the world would not be as beautiful or as fun. People are like flowers; the world needs all the different kinds to be beautiful and fun, so I appreciate and respect everyone, even if I don't like or agree with everything they do or say.

# I SEE ME AS I WILL BE.

I take time to visualize the life I want. As I lay in bed at night, I imagine what my perfect life will look like from the moment I wake up until I go to sleep. I see my future family, the house of my dreams, and I see myself doing the things I will do to make the world a better place. I imagine my perfect life as if I'm already living it, not watching it happen from the outside. It's hard at first, but I practice every night in bed, and it gets easier. Then I fall asleep and let my subconscious mind figure out how to make it happen. Together with my heart, my mind helps me get a little closer every day to the me I intend to be.

# I DO WHAT I FEEL AND KNOW IS RIGHT.

I follow my heart. I always listen to the small voice inside me, and do what feels right. I won't do something just because someone expects me to, or because it's what everyone else is doing, and I will never feel bad for following my heart. Even the person closest to me can't see my path. No one else has ever walked the path I must walk in life, but my heart lights the way.

# I AM ALWAYS LEARNING AND GROWING.

I learn something from every experience I have. I pay attention to the things that happen in my life every day because I know everything happens for me, and can teach me something about life or myself. I can learn something from everyone, even if I don't like everything they do or say. By paying attention to my feelings and what goes on around me all day long, I am always learning and growing.

# I DANCE TO THE RHYTHM OF LIFE.

Everything is energy, and energy is always in motion. There is a rhythm, a flow in life, and it's all around us: day flows into night; each season flows into the next; living things grow; new things get old; the moon goes through phases. I know there is a time for everything, and everything changes. When things change, I don't get upset; I just accept the change and explore what's new, so I can enjoy all it has to offer before it's gone. I love dancing to the rhythm of life!

# I AM ALWAYS IN THE RIGHT PLACE AT THE RIGHT TIME.

Nothing ever happens to me. Everything happens *for* me. Knowing everything happens for my good, I always pay attention to what's happening. Even if I don't like what's happening, I pay attention and notice how it makes me feel, rather than just wish it wasn't happening. That helps me learn from my experiences and get smarter. If I don't learn, life may repeat the experience over and over again. I am always in the right place at the right time. All I have to do is pay attention.

# I AM RESPONSIBLE FOR MY OWN HAPPINESS.

I am responsible for my own happiness. No one else can make me happy. I choose what I think, what I believe, and how I feel. What someone else thinks or feels is not my fault or my responsibility, and no one else is responsible for what I think or feel.

# I AM HAPPY SPENDING TIME OUTDOORS.

Outdoors is a wonderful place to be. I love the earth, the sky, the wind, the sea; I love the birds, the squirrels, bunnies and bees; I love the grass, the leaves, flowers, and trees. I love watching the sunrise and sunset, and splashing in puddles 'til I'm all wet; making snow angels before snowball fights, and staring at the stars and moon at night. I love being outdoors, breathing fresh air, with all of nature's beauty everywhere.

# I AM WRITING THE STORY OF ME.

With every thought I have, everything I believe, and everything I do, I am writing the story of me. I choose who I will be and the life I will live. I choose who and what is important in my story. Every day, I am writing my story, and I can change it anytime I choose to.

# I AM STILL COMPLETE!

I was born complete. I don't need anyone to complete me or tell me how I should be. All I need to be is me, and that means following my heart, not someone else. It's not easy, but I have the courage to love and respect myself. I was born complete, and I still am!

# I AM GRATEFUL FOR ANNOYING PEOPLE.

Sometimes, people do or say things I find upsetting or frustrating. What they are really doing is giving me an opportunity to be thoughtful and kind. When these things happen, I can stop thinking about myself, and think about what that person may be going through. Then I can take a deep breath, smile, and send that person loving thoughts. I know my thoughts and feelings are powerful, and how I think about things makes a big difference.

# I LIKE COMING TO MY SENSES.

My body is a living miracle. It has many senses which I enjoy taking time to experience and appreciate. I love to feel sunshine on my skin; I like to sit quietly and listen to all the sounds around me. I love the scent of freshly cut grass and the air after a thunderstorm. I love to look around my room and appreciate the things I have. I like to close my eyes and eat my favorite fruit slowly, allowing the juice, flavor, and texture to play on my tongue; listen to the sounds as I chew; and be thankful when I swallow and it goes into my stomach to give me nutrients I need to be healthy. I have many senses, and each is a blessing I'm very grateful for.

# I AM ME, HAPPILY!

I am me, happily, just as I am meant to be. I am true to myself, not a copy of someone else. I do my very best each day, happily me in every way.

# I ASK FOR HELP WHEN I NEED IT.

I like to do things by myself when I can, but some things I can't do alone. Everyone needs help sometimes, so I am not ashamed to ask for help when I need it, and I'm always happy to help others when I can.

# I ALWAYS WIN.

Things won't always go the way I want them to. I won't always get what I want, and some days are not going to be easy. Those things happen to everyone, and none of them matters. What matters is that I do my best even when things are hard, and that I am loving especially when I'm hurt, angry, or disappointed. What matters is that I believe everything happens for my good, even when I can't see it. What matters is that I bravely go through and grow through whatever I need to, so I'm always stronger, smarter, and ready for whatever comes next. That's how I always win.

# I AM NICE AND STRONG.

I am nice, but that doesn't mean I'm weak. I choose to be kind and thoughtful, but I also know I deserve to be respected and treated fairly. I will not let anyone treat me badly, take me for granted, or take advantage of my kindness. I love myself enough to take care of myself, and to not let others take advantage of me.

# *I AM ALL THIS AND MORE!*

I am
adorable, awesome, and amazing;
brave, blessed, and blissful;
calm, creative, and capable;
divine, delightful, and dependable;
empowered, exciting, and exceptional;
fair, fun, and fearless;
gifted, grateful, and glorious;
happy, healthy, and helpful;
intelligent, interesting, and inspired;
just, joyful, and jubilant;
kind, careful, and compassionate;
loving, loved, and love;
mindful, marvelous, and magnificent;
nice, neat, and noble;
obedient, optimistic, and outgoing;
peaceful, positive, and perfect;
quiet, quick, and questioning;
radiant, respectful, and reliable;
safe, smart, and sacred;
thoughtful, treasured, and thriving;
understanding, unique, and unstoppable;
vibrant, valued, and valiant;
wise, worthy, and wonderful;
excellent, exceptional, and extraordinary;
young, youthful, and euphoric;
zany, zealous, and zestful!

# I KNOW IT'S ALL GOOD.

It's hard to believe sometimes, but everything does happen for a reason. There are no accidents or mistakes. Earth is just the right distance from the sun; my organs all work every single second of my life to keep me alive without me even thinking about it; flowers never oversleep in spring; rain never falls up and goes off into space. Everything is perfect in the world, and that means everything is perfect in my life …even when it doesn't seem like it. Every experience I have is exactly what I need to help me become the person I'm here to be, to do what only I am here to do. Everything happens for a reason, and it's all good!

# I AM WHO I BELIEVE I AM!

I am unique. There has never been anyone like me, and there never will be. I am here to do something no one has ever done, which only I can do. That's why I won't let anyone tell me who to be, and I won't try to be like anyone else. I also won't let anyone tell me what's possible or what's impossible. They know what's been done and what hasn't been done yet, but no one know what I'm here to do. No one knows what I am capable of. With my beliefs, I am creating my life; I am who I believe I am.

"The only person
you were destined to
become is the person
you decide to be."

– Ralph Waldo Emerson

# HOW TO WRITE YOUR OWN AFFIRMATIONS.

Thank you for reading and thinking about those affirmations. Now that you understand what affirmations are, why they're important, and how they work, you can write your very own! Everyone is unique, and no one else knows your dreams like you do. That means you are the very best person to write the affirmations which will help you make your dreams come true.

At the beginning of this book, I said everyone does affirmations every day. That should make writing them easy, right? Well…

yes

…and no.

Because everyone does them every day, writing affirmations is easy. Writing ones that work, however, is not as simple as it may seem. It's definitely not difficult, but there are guidelines to follow in order to write powerful and effective affirmations.

Effective affirmations help you achieve what you are affirming. Remember, affirmations as we use them are not simply statements which reflect your current reality; they are tools you use to create the reality you want to experience.

## Guidelines for writing effective affirmations.

<u>Use present tense.</u>

The first guideline to remember is that you create your future reality by affirming it in the present tense. This is important because to your sub-conscious mind, there is no past or future; time doesn't exist, so it's always now. Effective affirmations need to be said as if they are already true. This is what causes the conflict your subconscious mind will be forced to resolve when the affirmation doesn't match the reality you're currently experiencing. Your subconscious mind always accepts the stronger of two conflicting thoughts or ideas without question or judgement. It will have no choice but to start changing the reality outside to match the message inside if that message is repeated often enough. Remember it's your subconscious mind that's quietly running the show in the background. It takes care of things which seem to happen automatically such as breathing, your heart beating, walking, and even suddenly remembering something you had been trying to remember since yesterday. It controls at least 95% of your life, so when you learn to direct it through the use of affirmations, you can truly create the life you want.

Use "I am".

The second guideline is to use the words "I am" whenever you can. This helps keep the affirmation in the present tense, but much more important is the fact that "I am" are the two most powerful words in the English language. Everything you add to "I am" becomes a command to your subconscious mind.

Stay positive

Guideline number three is to keep your affirmations positive. This is important because your subconscious mind only understands positive statements. It ignores words like "not", "don't", "can't", "won't" etc., so whatever you do, please don't think of a dog.

You thought of a dog, didn't you?

I knew it!

Your subconscious mind communicates through feelings and images. Even when you put a negative word in front of something, your mind creates an image of that thing. Always find a positive way of saying what you want, because you will get what you focus on.

<u>Be specific</u>

The fourth guideline is to be specific. Most people don't know exactly what they want; they tend to be unclear about their dreams, then get frustrated when they don't get exactly what they want. Not being specific when you order a meal at a restaurant could lead to a disappointing experience unless you get lucky. Just asking for "something nice" for your birthday is more likely to get you something you didn't want than exactly what you were hoping for. Affirmations are the same way; they work best when you know exactly what you want and remain focused on just that. It is also a good idea to focus on affirmations which feel natural to you, or at least possible. Affirming something impossible or completely unnatural for you (for example, "I walk on the ocean" or "I have a gazillion dollars") won't work. Instead, it will only lead to stress and disappointment as your mind tries to resolve a conflict such as how to walk on water, which it knows is impossible, or exactly how much is a "gazillion".

<u>Keep it short and simple.</u>

Guideline number five is to keep it short and simple. This may seem like a challenge after number four, but keeping an affirmation short and simple makes it easy for you to remember and repeat, and easy for your subconscious mind to start working on.

<u>Feel it!</u>

The sixth guideline is to get emotional. Because your subconscious mind communicates through feelings and images, it's helpful to include how you will feel when what you are affirming becomes real. If you will feel happy, you can start with "I'm so happy I am…" and say it as if you really are happy. Imagine how you will feel when it's real, and act as if it already is. It might feel weird or fake at first, but your subconscious mind can't tell the difference between what's real and what's not. That's why you wake up from nightmares screaming and sweating with your heart racing, even when you are safe in your own bed. The more real you make your affirmations feel, the better and sooner they will work.

<u>Action!</u>

Finally, you may add even more detail to your affirmations by including some action. Imagine the experience you will have when it becomes real, and include something you will do. Perhaps "I am waving to my mother in the front row as I proudly walk across the stage to accept The Nobel Peace Prize."

Now you are ready to write your very own positive and powerful affirmations which you can use to help you be exactly who you want to be, and create the life you want to have. On the following page, you will find some space to get started writing your own affirmations!

# MY AFFIRMATIONS.

________________________________________

________________________________________

________________________________________

________________________________________

________________________________________

________________________________________

________________________________________

________________________________________

________________________________________

________________________________________

________________________________________

________________________________________

Thank you for reading this book. If you enjoyed it and found it helpful, please tell a friend about it if you think your friend might enjoy it and find it helpful too. You may also go to www.amazon.com/author/meforbes and leave a review of this book. By doing so, you will be helping others know about this book and how it could help them. You will also be letting Amazon know you like the book, which may cause them to show it to other readers who may like it.

Again, thank you very much. Remember, you are precious, you are very much loved, and you will do amazing things.

Sincerely,

M.